MW01611500

Catholic Journal Meditation & Mental Prayer

Acquiring the Sanctity Necessary for Salvation

BY

MANRESA PRESS

Table of Contents

Jesus tells us the only way to heaven is on the narrow road. Open the pages of this journal and take the first steps on your journey to heaven.

Your Own Table of Contents

list your important notes here

Introduction

If you want to get on the narrow road and squeeze through that narrow gate then you must practice Meditation and Mental Prayer and this Catholic Journal will help you.

This Catholic Journal, Meditation teaches you about the necessity of Catholic Mental Prayer; for the saints assure us, that Mental Prayer, is morally necessary for salvation.

This Journal invites you to practice Meditation, and Contemplation; it teaches you the methods used by the saints to achieve Mental Prayer which establishes a strong connection with the heart of the Divine.

In days, months and years to come your Journal will be a document you can use to remind yourself, of lessons learned. It is easy to forget those light bulb moments when the words of Christ become real and resonate within your soul. Documenting these incidents is imperative in building a relationship with God. Reviewing these graces gives you an opportunity for thanksgiving and recommitment to God.

The Journal helps with setting up a "rule of life". Journaling about your Meditations allows you to plot and plan your prayer journey into the Heart of God. It stops you wandering about aimlessly in your mind.

Committing to it's use awakens you from spiritual drowsiness. This is how you overcome the rattling brain. The never ending imaginary conversations and the inane speculations.

In Silence, Mental Prayer, is God's way of helping the soul to overcome mortal sin and venial sin and even eradicate the *'tendency'* toward sin.

St John of the Cross tells us: "God desires the smallest degree of purity of conscience in you, more than all the works you can perform".

Practicing the "Presence of God" is part of the Meditation process. The Journal will keep recalling you to practice this spiritual art.

The goal then is to overcome your "Predominant Fault". Because loving God so much you want to do His will, which is, to know, love and serve Him here on earth and to be happy with Him for ever in Heaven.

"If you love me, keep my commandments." Even the smallest infringement you will discover is an insult to the all Loving God.

Why then do the saints contend that Mental prayer, is morally necessary for salvation? Why "morally" necessary? Because coming so close to God in Mental Prayer our smallest faults are magnified in the light of His loving grace. Without Mental Prayer this doesn't happen.

St Alphonsus Liguori tells us, "In the first place, without mental prayer the soul is without light." and "It is morally impossible for him who neglects meditation, to live without sin."

St. Augustine says that those who, "Keep their eyes shut cannot see the way to their country. The eternal truths are all spiritual things that are seen, not with eyes of the body, but with the eyes of the mind; that is, by reflection and consideration. Now, they, who do not make mental prayer, do not see these truths, neither do they see the importance of eternal salvation, and the means which they can adopt in order to obtain it."

St Teresa of Avila tells us: "Mental prayer in my opinion is nothing else than an intimate sharing between friends; it means taking time frequently to be alone with Him, who we know loves us. The important thing is not to think much but to love much and so do that which best stirs you to love. Love is not great delight but desire to please God in everything." Again: - "If you love me, keep my commandments"

"What then can arouse us from this wretched sluggishness, if not the practice of mental prayer? Little by little mental prayer, well made, will render our faith more lively, will strengthen our convictions, will penetrate us deeply with the things of God. It will keep the supernatural always present to our mind." (Vitalis Lehodey OCR)

To expedite our faults is our <u>first objective</u> in Mental Prayer

To know Jesus Christ more clearly, in order to love Him more dearly and to follow Him more nearly.

"What, more do you want, O soul!

And what else do you search for outside, when within yourself you possess your riches, delights, satisfactions, fullness, and kingdom - your Beloved whom you desire and seek?

Be joyful and gladdened in your interior recollection with Him, for you have Him so close to you.

Desire Him there, adore Him there. Do not go in pursuit of Him outside yourself. You will only become distracted and wearied thereby, and you shall not find Him, nor enjoy Him more securely, nor sooner, nor more intimately than by seeking Him within you." (St John of the Cross.)

Placing yourself in the Presence of God

Actively realise that the Presence of God is all around you. Outside look at the whole picture before you. The trees, grass, clouds. Know that God permeates them all. He is everywhere at once. He is there, through His Love and knowledge of all His created things. Before you begin your meditation "see" this same Holy Presence in the room all around you.
God's presence is more that just Being. His presence is the essence that keeps all things in reality. It is not that the world swirls around inside of God. No, God has command of it all. God oversees it. All things belong to Him. He created all. You belong to Him. The Supreme Being knows and Loves you intimately.

Present in His attributes
All God's attributes are present in His presence. He has wisdom of every minuscule atom of every living thing in the world. God is present in His "Providence" in that He provides existence for all. This providence isn't just something God does. He *IS*, providence.
God is nearer to us than the air we breathe and He was 'waiting' there before you took your first breath. Gently, effortlessly watch all this. Focus on it. Enjoy it. Enjoy God's Holy Presence.

Present in our hearts
Instead of looking outward, centre your attention within your body in the region of your heart realising it is His Presence in your heart that keeps it beating. His Presence there keeps you alive in this world and translates into the spiritual realm when you leave through "death".

In like manner, David calls Him the "strength of my heart"

The Presence of Jesus as a Friend
Every time during the day when you discover you are 'talking' in your imagination to a friend, replace the image of your friend with that of Jesus. Tell it to Him instead.:

"He that eateth my flesh, and drinketh my blood, abideth in me, and I in him."

EXAMPLE MEDITATION

St Teresa of Avila tells us that when she first started Mental Prayer she needed a book to help her but adds that, later she had no need of any stimulus.

Scripture Reading
A chosen piece of scripture is read and is meditated upon in three parts. Used on retreats and private prayer, these would be divided into morning, noon and evening meditations. The meditations are called **"Considerations"**.

Having 'considered' or meditated upon the implications of the short piece of scripture we are then directed to consider its **"Application"** to our own spiritual life. It is at this point that we move into Mental Prayer.

Affections and resolutions are the terms used in the final part of this type of guided mental prayer. The affection is for God and we show it through personal conversational prayer with Him. The Resolutions are decisions to overcome faults highlighted in the scripture we just read. Or, by Divine Guidance we received during the Mental Prayer.

For instance here is a meditation which uses the Shepherds of Bethlehem to make us consider the virtues of Humility, Poverty and Mortification

The shepherds of Bethlehem Read: Luke 2. 8-14

First consideration
Consider firstly in what way the birth of Christ was made known to the shepherds by the angels. They were surrounded by a bright light and were seized by great fear; Then great joy was announced to the shepherds, because the birth of the saviour of the world. Such is the way in which Almighty God prepares souls to receive spiritual favours; he illuminates their intellect, and at the same time awakes and sends into the heart a deeper reverence and holy fear.

Application to your own life
There is indeed great cause for joy when Jesus is born spiritually in a heart. What real joy will there be at Christmas unless the holy infant be born in your heart by love and by Grace.

Reflections and resolutions
My heart shall rejoice in my salvation I Will sing unto the Lord who has given me good things (ps 12:7)

Second consideration Secondly consider the sign that was given to the shepherds that they might find the divine infant; *"you shall find the infant wrapped in swaddling clothes and laid in a manger."*

The child would be clad in the poorest of garments, lying, in a manger normally used for animal feed.

Application to your own life.
Reflect on the fact that this is the only way you will find Jesus, namely in humility, poverty and mortification. If you seek Him by another way with goals of ambition, of comforts, or of attachment to worldly goods: you will not find Jesus. But if you work to acquire the virtues of humility, poverty and mortification, there will be sure signs of the holy infant being born in your heart.

Affections and resolutions
Turn away my eyes less they hold vanity. (ps. 118:37). How do you feel when a neighbour, friend, or enemy finds you in your worst embarrassing situation? Do you mentally join with the Holy Family at Bethlehem and be glad? Rethink similar situations in your life.

Third Consideration
The song the angels were singing when they appeared to the shepherds:
Glory to God in the highest and peace to men of good will. The Babe at Bethlehem came for two reasons: Firstly to proclaim the glory of God and secondly for the good of mankind. God announced the birth of His Son by sending multitudes of His heavenly messengers to announce the glad tidings to these simple, poor shepherds.

Application
The greater glory of God should be your sole objective in your life and all your work. All you do and all you are, should be directed to the glory of God not keeping for yourself anything that belongs by right to God. To God alone the honour and glory. You should seek to make peace with God through the pardon of your sins. Make peace with yourself by conquering the flesh, and peace with your neighbour by real charity.

Finally this piece is not so much for men of great intellect or natural gifts. As for men of goodwill who strive to conform themselves to the example set them by Jesus and to imitate the virtues taught in his birth.

Affection and resolutions
Not onto us oh lord, not on to us, but onto thy name give glory (ps.113:7)

---

* Should you for any reason not be able to do your mental prayer in the morning it should be done some time later in the day. It is our duty as Christians to come into His presence every day.

Sample: The Presence of God

"Holy Ghost enlighten and help me."

"Spirit of the Living God, fall afresh on me."

Focus, relax, love Jesus. Meditate on:

God all around me. God in and through me.
God keeping me alive. God in my breath. God
at the centre of my being.

Christ standing on my right side watching me.

Christ with me, Christ before me, Christ behind me, Christ in me,

Christ beneath me, Christ above me, Christ on my right, Christ on my left,

Christ when I lie down, Christ when I sit down, Christ when I arise.

Christ waiting: waiting to converse with me.
Christ before me. Knowing and loving me.
I lower my eyes in humility and love in return.

"In You I live and move and have
my being"

Virtue to Aquire   **Temperance and Charity (love of God)**

Predominant Fault to overcome
Constant chattering in my mind all day every day

Because of my love for God I make these resolutions…

Jesus gave me grace today to see how my mind is constantly filled with chatter.

Talking to imaginary people, instead of talking to Him.
"Seek ye first the kingdom of God".
"First I am the Lord thy God.".

Jesus shows me He wants to be First in my life, all day every-day.
What can I do, to still this inane chatter in my mind?
From now on I will . . . .

Lord thank you for

The first part of the thanksgiving can be done in silence. Try "talking" to God without using any words in your mind.
Show Him the gratitude welling up in your emotions without using any words.

Guided Meditation

Read Matt 13 v24 - 30.
Meditation and mental prayer
for the parable of the cockle and the good seed

First consideration
What abundant seeds of lights and good thoughts, impulses and holy inspirations God has sown in your mind.

Another person, being blessed to the same degree, would probably be a saint by now. Whereas you realise you have't even started on your journey through the narrow gate.

How much good wheat does God expect to find in you, when He considers all his special inspirations He imparted to you through the years? How many negligences have you been guilty of?

What sins have you unknowingly committed? What sins have you deliberately committed?

Examine carefully the kind of life you have been leading up until now. Place along side it the gifts of grace which you have received from the hand of God. You'll be shocked at the discrepancy, between the graces given to you and the lack of fruit you have produced.

Second consideration
So how is it that we return to God a harvest of Cockle which is a harvest of sins in our lives? How is it, that we do not return to him a great beautiful harvest of wheat? Where are our virtues? As we come before Him in meditation what does He see when He looks at us?

Where does the cockle come from? The cockle comes from two sources. The first is our own fault and the second is the malice of our enemies.

The person who is asleep has his eyes closed because he is caring for his body. But he is unconscious to the needs of his soul.

When you do not engage in mental prayer you are like that person sleeping with interest only in placating your senses.

This is the first cause of the growth of cockle.

The second cause is the malice of your mortal enemies who seeing you asleep and neglecting to keep in constant contact with God, never cease to assault you. Into your empty mind and misused imagination they sow worldly thoughts, suggestions and desires enticing you into evil.

Be vigilant and watch over yourself. Always remember that these enemies, never ever sleep.

Third considerations
We must admit that the good seed cannot at first be easily distinguished from the bad seed, In early growth it is hard to distinguish the cockle from the wheat, but after harvest they are quickly recognised.

In the same way, in this life where the virtuous live together with sinners; the holy with the lukewarm; the more perfect with the less perfect, it is not always easy to distinguish the one from the other. Furthermore in one person what presents as a virtue might stem from a less than virtuous motivation.

On judgement day the Divine Husbandman will order the good seed to be separated from the cockle; vice from virtue; the reprobate from the elect. One will be consigned to Hell the other welcomed into Heaven.

Jesus says: "Gather up first the cockle and bind into bundles, to burn but gather the wheat into my barn." What a terrible separation that will be–the separation of the reprobate into an eternal fire, and of the elect to the glory of paradise.

Remember that you also remain ever exposed to this separation even onto the last moment of your life. Recall how St Teresa of Avila was taken to Hell and shown the terrible place Satan had awaiting her should she die in mortal sin.

Always recall this thought seriously and frequently in your heart.

How to use the Journaling Pages

To expedite our faults is our first objective in Mental Prayer

The Journaling pages are in sets of two for each meditation. The first page is odd numbered, on the right, while the second page is even numbered on the back of it.

On the the lined page your personal colloquy or prayer can be written. If during your mental prayer you happen to euphorically promise God something - best to record it here. Once in a while, read back through your Journal pages to pick up again these often forgotten promises!

At the bottom left of the page is a place to note the pre-dominant fault that you are addressing at the moment. Here also can be recorded a virtue you wish to acquire.

An examination of conscience is on page 127 to help you identify faults you may have overlooked.

The even numbered pages are self explanatory. Basically you record the outcome of your meditation and mental prayer in the first section.

In the bottom panel write a thank you for all the graces received. Don't forget to give thanks also for the wealth of material gifts God bestows on us daily.

The guided verses are short but if you feel the Holy Spirit calling you to read more of the chapter then of course do so. Mental Prayer is about attaining an intimate life with Jesus Christ.

Page 101 gives you an opportunity to make a short meditation on virtues and vices.

Beginning on page 120 there is a six week Meditation Planner. Use these for Lent or for a personal dedicated retreat.

Finally on page 177 there is a chance to Contemplate God in His attributes. God cannot be divided up but our human way of listing and describing His perfections if meditated upon brings great joy and an etherial dimension to our spirituality.

What Catholic Meditation and Mental Prayer is Not:

Often Catholics ask, "are we allowed to Meditate?" or "Is Meditation dangerous to a Catholic?" Here are some meditation techniques that should be avoided by all Catholics.

Catholic meditation is not transcendental meditation which uses a one word mantra repeated over and over in order to subdue the thoughts. In the first place this type of meditation is New Age and secondly it is badly copied from Hindu religion. This, of course, renders it totally inappropriate for Christian use.

It is not meditation to relax you. The purpose is not to lull you to sleep or rid you of anxiety. Although it may well have this side-effect, this is not the goal.

It is not to give you confidence. The purpose is not to fill you with grandiose ideas about yourself. Rather the opposite is the intention because in meeting God we realise how dependant we are on Him.

It is not Centering prayer. Centering prayer has recently become popular in some Catholic circles but has been identified as 'dangerous' in others. This is because the 'finding of oneself within' and a 'sense of the other' is taken from Buddhist philosophy. It's the 'other' that is the problem.

It is not mental gymnastics trying to still the mind and lead it to nothingness. There is no "nothing" except perhaps in hell. God is coming, we need to be alert and thinking of Him.

It is not Pantheism. Pantheism is the belief that everything is God. There is no distinct personal God. I recall a woman pointing to a tree and saying to me, "That's God." Satan loves Pantheism and you can understand why. The reason I mention it here is because the goal, to be always in the presence of God has its foundation in St Paul's statement. "In you I live and move and have my being." Also our Catechism answer to the question, "Where is God?" is "God is everywhere…" might lead people to see it as Pantheism however the complete answer is "but in a special way he is in heaven where he is seen by the angels and saints."

This is our God. The one true God, creator and maker of all things visible and invisible. He knows us intimately and loves us immensely. Through Catholic Mental Prayer we will come to know and love Him immensely in return.

Read Luke 11:13 "If you then, being evil, know how to give good gifts to your children, how much more will your Father from heaven give the good Spirit to them that ask him?"

Virtue to Aquire

Predominant Fault to overcome

Because of my love for God I make these resolutions…

_____

_____

_____

_____

_____

_____

_____

_____

_____

_____

Lord thank you for

Read Mark 12:30 "And thou shalt love the Lord thy God, with thy whole heart, and with thy whole soul, and with thy whole mind, and with thy whole strength. This is the first commandment."

Virtue to Aquire

Predominant Fault to overcome

Because of my love for God I make these resolutions…

Thanks-giving

Read Matt 19:17 "Who said to him: Why asketh thou me concerning good? One is good, God. But if thou wilt enter into life, keep the commandments."

Virtue to Aquire

Predominant Fault to overcome

Because of my love for God I make these resolutions…

_____

_____

_____

_____

_____

_____

_____

_____

_____

_____

Thank you Lord for…

Read John 14:21He that hath my commandments, and keepeth them; he it is that loveth me. And he that loveth me, shall be loved of my Father: and I will love him, and will manifest myself to him."

Virtue to Aquire

Predominant Fault to overcome

Because of my love for God I
make these resolutions…

_____

_____

_____

_____

_____

_____

_____

_____

_____

_____

Thank you Lord for…

St Alphonsus Liguori

St. Alphonsus Marie Liguori is one of the
greatest saints the Church. As well as Poverty,
Chastity and Obedience, he took a fourth vow
to never be idle. He was bishop, missionary
and founder of the Redemptorist Order. His
feast day in the Latin Mass Calendar is on
August 2.

Practicing the Presence of God was most important to St Alphonsus Liguori. He says:

"There is a practice that is most powerful in keeping us united with God. That practice is the constant recollection of His presence."

Mental Prayer consists in conversing with God in a familiar way. We discuss the scripture we are reading. We listen to His side of things. This comes in different ways. As a deep rush of understanding. A warmth that makes us smile at God. A stab of shock as we are enlightened by Him to a serious fault we commit.

St Alphonsus says:

"Acquire the habit of speaking to God as if you were alone with Him, familiarly and with confidence and love, as to the dearest and most loving of friends. Speak to Him often of your business, your plans, your troubles, your fears - of everything that concerns you. Converse with Him confidently and frankly; for God is not wont to speak to a soul that does not speak to Him."

When we read what St Alphonsus says about those saved and those who are not saved we can better understand those shocking statements made by the saints. Without the Practice of Mental Prayer it is impossible to be morally worthy to enter heaven.

"Whoever prays is certainly saved. He who does not is certainly damned. All the blessed have been saved by prayer. All the damned have been lost through not praying. If they had prayed they would not have been lost. And this is, and will be their greatest torment in hell: to think how easily they might have been saved, just by asking God for His grace. Now they are too late - their time of prayer is gone."

How often do we doubt this and presume on God's mercy? While doing very little ourselves to bend our lives to God's will."

Practice of the Presence of God awakens our soul to true reality. The spiritual life of the soul becomes weak and jaundiced if we do not practice Mental Prayer.

Read Matt 5:44 "But I say to you, Love your enemies: do good to them that hate you: and pray for them that persecute and calumniate you."

Virtue to Aquire

Predominant Fault to overcome

Because of my love for God I
make these resolutions…

_____

_____

_____

_____

_____

_____

_____

_____

_____

_____

_____

Thank you Lord for…

Read Matt 6:24. "No man can serve two masters. For either he will hate the one, and love the other: or he will sustain the one, and despise the other. You cannot serve God and mammon."

Virtue to Aquire

Predominant Fault to overcome

Because of my love for God I make these resolutions…

_____

_____

_____

_____

_____

_____

_____

_____

_____

Thank you Lord for…

Read Matt 10:37   "He that loveth father or mother more than me, is not worthy of me; and he that loveth son or daughter more than me, is not worthy of me."

Virtue to Aquire

Predominant Fault to overcome

Because of my love for God I make these resolutions…

_____

_____

_____

_____

_____

_____

_____

_____

_____

_____

Thank you Lord for…

They put on Him His own garments and led Him away to crucify Him
Matt. 27:31. Jesus receives the cross with humble
resignation, He conformed Himself perfectly to the Father's Will.

Virtue to Aquire

Predominant Fault to overcome

Because of my love for God I make these resolutions…

_____

_____

_____

_____

_____

_____

_____

_____

_____

Thank you Lord for…

"And going out, they found a man of Cyrene named Simon: him they forced to take up his cross" Matt. 27, 32 The cross to Simon was a shame and ignominy. Forced, Simon did help Jesus carry the cross. Our crosses are repugnant, coming in sickness, in the cares and worries of or daily life.

Virtue to Aquire

Predominant Fault to overcome

Because of my love for God I make these resolutions…

_____

_____

_____

_____

_____

_____

_____

_____

_____

_____

Thank you Lord for…

The Four Last Things: Death; Judgment; Heaven; Hell. "The Son of Man will render every man according to his works." Matt 16:27. "In all thy works remember thy last end and thou shalt never sin." Ecclus. 7:40

Virtue to Aquire

Predominant Fault to overcome

Because of my love for God I make these resolutions…

_____

_____

_____

_____

_____

_____

_____

_____

_____

Thank you Lord for…

"If any man will come after me, let him deny himself, and take up his cross daily and follow me."   Luke 9:23. "They that are Christ's have crucified their flesh" Gal. 5:24

Virtue to Aquire

Predominant Fault to overcome

Because of my love for God I make these resolutions…

_____

_____

_____

_____

_____

_____

_____

_____

_____

_____

Thank you Lord for…

"Then shall He say to them also that shall be on His left hand: Depart from me, ye cursed, into everlasting fire." Mat 25:41. "Pierce thou my flesh with fear: for I am afraid of thy judgements." Ps. 118:120.

Virtue to Aquire

Predominant Fault to overcome

Because of my love for God I make these resolutions…

_____

_____

_____

_____

_____

_____

_____

_____

_____

Thank you Lord for…

"All whatsoever ye do, in word or in work, all things do ye in the name of the Lord Jesus Christ."   Col.3:17. "Every day will I bless thee: and I will praise thy name for ever. Yea for ever and ever." Ps. cxliv.2)

Virtue to Aquire

Predominant Fault to overcome

Because of my love for God I make these resolutions…

_____

_____

_____

_____

_____

_____

_____

_____

_____

_____

Thank you Lord for…

"My soul doth magnify the Lord. And my spirit hath rejoiced in God my Saviour." Luke 1:46

Virtue to Aquire

Predominant Fault to overcome

Because of my love for God I make these resolutions…

_____

_____

_____

_____

_____

_____

_____

_____

_____

_____

Thank you Lord for…

"He that is faithful in that which is least is faithful also in that which is greater." Luke 16.10 "Thy word is a lamp to my feet, and a light to my paths. I have sworn, and am determined to keep the judgments of thy justice." Ps.118: 105,106.

Virtue to Aquire

Predominant Fault to overcome

Because of my love for God I
make these resolutions…

_____

_____

_____

_____

_____

_____

_____

_____

_____

_____

Thank you Lord for…

"And suddenly there was with the angel a multitude of the heavenly army, praising God, and saying: Glory to God in the highest; and on earth peace to men of good will." Luke 2:13-14

Virtue to Aquire

Predominant Fault to overcome

Because of my love for God I make these resolutions…

_____

_____

_____

_____

_____

_____

_____

_____

_____

_____

Thank you Lord for…

St. Ignatius Loyola

Born in 1491 at the castle of Loyola in Spain he died at Rome, 31 July 1556. He co-founded the religious order of the Society of Jesus (Jesuits) as its first Superior General. The order served the Pope as missionaries and were bound by a vow of special obedience to the sovereign pontiff in regard to the missions.

St. Ignatius Loyola

St Ignatius says: "For it is not to know much, but it is to understand and savour the matter interiorly that fills and satisfies the soul"

In meditation we use our memory, understanding and will to examine the mysteries and truths of our holy faith. We reflect within ourselves, talking to God as a good friend. As a Father to us, we beg Him for his gifts of grace. He guides us to understand, what is necessary for our salvation and perfection.

"The masters of the spiritual life commonly teach that the following is what we have to observe in all our prayer, namely, that we are not to spend the whole time in merely meditating and reflecting upon the subject we have in hand.

It is chiefly necessary that we move our will with affections and desires which are formed first of all in the heart, in order that they may produce their fruit in due time and may be put into execution."

St Ignatius wrote Spiritual Exercises which were so powerful that his friend Francis Xavier was converted after meditating upon them. To this day they are used in silent retreats.

"Ad majorem dei Gloriam"

For the greater glory of God.

Blessed are the clean of heart: for they shall
see God. Matt 5:8

Virtue to Aquire

Predominant Fault to overcome

Because of my love for God I make these resolutions…

_____

_____

_____

_____

_____

_____

_____

_____

_____

_____

_____

Thank you Lord for…

But I say unto you, that every idle word that men shall speak, they shall render an account for it in the day of judgment. Matt 12:36

Virtue to Aquire

Predominant Fault to overcome

Because of my love for God I make these resolutions…

_____

_____

_____

_____

_____

_____

_____

_____

_____

Thank you Lord for…

"For by thy words thou shalt be justified, and by thy words thou shalt be condemned."
Matt 12:37

Virtue to Aquire

Predominant Fault to overcome

Because of my love for God I make these resolutions…

_____

_____

_____

_____

_____

_____

_____

_____

_____

_____

Thank you Lord for…

"For from within the heart of men proceed evil thoughts, adulter-ies, fornications, murders, Thefts, covetousness, wickedness, deceit, lasciviousness, an evil eye, blasphemy, pride, foolish-ness. All these evil things come from within, and defile a man."
Mark 7:21

Virtue to Aquire

Predominant Fault to overcome

Because of my love for God I
make these resolutions…

_____

_____

_____

_____

_____

_____

_____

_____

_____

_____

Thank you Lord for…

"Let nothing be done through contention, neither by vain glory: but by humility, let each esteem others better than themselves." Phil 2:3

Virtue to Aquire

Predominant Fault to overcome

Because of my love for God I
make these resolutions…

_____

_____

_____

_____

_____

_____

_____

_____

_____

_____

Thank you Lord for…

"Wherefore, my dearly beloved, with fear and trembling work out your salvation. And do ye all things without murmurings and hesitation." Phil 12:15

Virtue to Aquire

Predominant Fault to overcome

Because of my love for God I make these resolutions…ed;

_____

_____

_____

_____

_____

_____

_____

_____

_____

_____

Thank you Lord for…

"Put on then, as God's chosen ones, holy and beloved, compassionate hearts, kindness, humility, meekness, and patience." Cols 3:2

Virtue to Aquire

Predominant Fault to overcome

Because of my love for God I make these resolutions…

_____

_____

_____

_____

_____

_____

_____

_____

_____

_____

Thank you Lord for…

"And being found in human form, he humbled himself by becoming obedient to the point of death, even death on a cross." Phil 2:8

Virtue to Aquire

Predominant Fault to overcome

Because of my love for God I make these resolutions…

_____

_____

_____

_____

_____

_____

_____

_____

_____

Thank you Lord for…

"In all things give thanks; for this is the will of God
in Christ Jesus concerning you." 1 Thes 5:18

Virtue to Aquire

Predominant Fault to overcome

Because of my love for God I make these resolutions…

_____

_____

_____

_____

_____

_____

_____

_____

_____

_____

Thank you Lord for…

"Let the word of Christ swell in you abundantly, in all wisdom: teaching and admonishing one another in psalms hymns and spiritual canticles, singing in grace in your hearts to God. All whatsoever you do in word or in work, do all in the name of the Lord Jesus Christ, giving thanks to God and the Father by Him."

Virtue to Aquire

Predominant Fault to overcome

Because of my love for God I make these resolutions…

_____

_____

_____

_____

_____

_____

_____

_____

_____

_____

Thank you Lord for…

Read Matt21.1-10: Consider the triumph of Jesus as He goes toward the Cross.He called it an exaltation. How often are we fickle tell God we love and adore Him and the next sinning against Him.

Virtue to Aquire

Predominant Fault to overcome

Because of my love for God I
make these resolutions...

_____

_____

_____

_____

_____

_____

_____

_____

_____

Thank you Lord for...

St. John of The Cross

Founder (with St. Teresa) of the Discalced
Carmelites, doctor of mystic theology, he was
born at Hontoveros, Old Castile, 24 June, 1542;
and died at Ubeda, Andalusia, 14 Dec., 1591

St John of the Cross tells us:

"Without the aid of Mental Prayer, the soul cannot triumph over the forces of the demon."

Love consists not in feeling great things but in having great detachment and in suffering for the Beloved.

Live as though only God and yourself were in this world, so that your heart may not be detained by anything human.

Contemplation is nothing else but a secret, peaceful and loving infusion of God, which if admitted, will set the soul on fire with the Spirit of love.

What we need most in order to make progress is to be silent before this great God with our appetite and with our tongue, for the language he best hears is silent love.

God is awakened in the soul. God breathes in the soul. Oh, how happy is this soul that is ever conscious of God resting and reposing within its breast!

The very pure spirit does not bother about the regard of others or human respect, but communes inwardly with God, alone and in solitude and with delightful tranquility, for the knowledge of God is received in divine silence.

Feast of the Holy Name of Jesus "For there is no other name under heaven given to men whereby we must be saved". Acs 4:12

Example Meditation

Readings: **Luke 2:21.** And after eight days were accomplished, that the child should be circumcised, his name was called JESUS, which was called by the angel, before he was conceived in the womb."

Psalm 78:9 "Help us, O God, our saviour: and for the glory of thy name, O Lord, deliver us: and forgive us our sins for thy name's sake" **Phil 2:10** "That in the name of Jesus every knee should bow, of those that are in heaven, on earth, and under the earth"

Habakkuk 3:18 "But I will rejoice in the Lord: and I will have joy in God my Jesus."

Why do you not have recourse to JESUS and invoke this Holy Name in all your needs and temptations, your labours and dangers, availing yourself of this name as a shield to defend you against the attacks of the enemy, as comfort and to soothe you in your labours, as a light to rescue you from dangers?

Consider that the first time that this life giving and most Holy Name, which was decreed by the Father, was pronounced by a human being: it came from the lips of the Blessed Virgin, who as she uttered it, was overwhelmed with sweetness and with joy.

Virtue to Aquire

Predominant Fault to overcome

Because of my love for God I make these resolutions…

_____

_____

_____

_____

_____

_____

_____

_____

_____

_____

Thank you Lord for…

Read John 19:28,29. "I thirst" He cried out letting us know how He suffered for our sins of intemperance and gluttony. His death on a cross was by the Will of the Divine Father. Will the ransom He paid for you be to no avail.

Virtue to Aquire

Predominant Fault to overcome

Because of my love for God I make these resolutions…

_____
_____
_____
_____
_____
_____
_____
_____
_____
_____

Thank you Lord for…

Read John.19:30 Jesus had finish His life on earth every moment of which He had done His duty according to the Will of the Father. Will you on your death bed feel the same.

Virtue to Aquire

Predominant Fault to overcome

Because of my love for God I make these resolutions…

_____

_____

_____

_____

_____

_____

_____

_____

_____

Thank you Lord for…

Read Matt 20:.19 "They shall deliver Him to the Gentiles to be mocked and scourged and crucified." Why are you not moved? He was atoning for your sins. He loves you so much.

Virtue to Aquire

Predominant Fault to overcome

Because of my love for God I make these resolutions…

_____

_____

_____

_____

_____

_____

_____

_____

_____

_____

Thank you Lord for…

Read Mark 15:37 The cry of Christ dying fills every creature with sorrow and echoes throughout the whole universe. So far what reparation have you made for your offences? "I am thy servant O Lord, give me understanding." Ps. 118:59-60

Virtue to Aquire

Predominant Fault to overcome

Because of my love for God I make these resolutions…

_____

_____

_____

_____

_____

_____

_____

_____

_____

Thank you Lord for…

Read Matt 27:59-60 Joseph taking the body wrapped it up in a clean linen cloth, and laid it in his own new monument. We too should keep Jesus in our hearts so that we may rise with Him each day in His Glory. Pray for the Church of which you are so necessary a part.

Virtue to Aquire

Predominant Fault to overcome

Because of my love for God I make these resolutions…

_____

_____

_____

_____

_____

_____

_____

_____

_____

Thank you Lord for…

Read Mark 16:1-7 Imagine the cry of joy the prophets and patriarchs gave at the sight of the Messiah as He came to be with them also in Limbo and release them into heaven. So too in Holy Communion He descends into your heart. How will that reception be?

Virtue to Aquire

Predominant Fault to overcome

Because of my love for God I
make these resolutions…

_____

_____

_____

_____

_____

_____

_____

_____

_____

_____

Thank you Lord for…

Read John 14:18 I will not leave you orphans. I will come to you. Can you ever comprehend the joy and love Our Lady felt when Jesus came to Her especially after all Her pain and suffering? Through your life's pains and suffering, if borne well, you will merit such great joy when you meet your Jesus at the gates of heaven.

Virtue to Aquire

Predominant Fault to overcome

Because of my love for God I
make these resolutions…

_____

_____

_____

_____

_____

_____

_____

_____

_____

_____

Thank you Lord for…

Read Mark 16:1-9 The holy women received a special grace. They were addressed by a holy angel with a message direct from God Himself. You too will merit special graces, if like them you follow His teaching, follow Him to Calvary and even to the tomb.

Virtue to Aquire

Predominant Fault to overcome

Because of my love for God I make these resolutions…

_____

_____

_____

_____

_____

_____

_____

_____

_____

Thank you Lord for…

Read Luke 24:34. The Lord is risen indeed and hath appeared to Simon. How did Simon feel when he saw Our Lord alive again. The last time they looked into each others eyes Peter had denied Him. But Jesus understood Peter's weakness and simply bid Peter confirm the other apostles. You cannot give up and despair, the Church needs you.

Virtue to Aquire

Predominant Fault to overcome

Because of my love for God I make these resolutions…

_____

_____

_____

_____

_____

_____

_____

_____

_____

Thank you Lord for…

Read John 20:10 When it was late the same day...Jesus came and stood in the midst. When you are impatient to receive graces remember how the apostles had to wait until "late" that day until they saw Jesus. Got teaches you through that waiting period important lessons, He knows you need to learn.

Virtue to Aquire

Predominant Fault to overcome

Because of my love for God I make these resolutions…

_____

_____

_____

_____

_____

_____

_____

_____

_____

_____

_____

_____

Thank you Lord for…

Read   John 21:1 Jesus showed himself again to the disciples at the sea of Tiberias.   They had fished all night and caught nothing. So many people "fish" for wealth and esteem and pass out of this world with no treasure for the next. In your work and daily duties do you work for the kingdom of God, mending the torn nets of your prideful behaviour and then through prayer "catching" souls for God.

Virtue to Aquire

Predominant Fault to overcome

Because of my love for God I make these resolutions…

_____
_____
_____
_____
_____
_____
_____
_____
_____
_____
_____

Thank you Lord for…

Acquiring Virtue through the Grace of God

Ponder the fact that God has made you a gardener, to root out vice and plant virtue.

Prudence

Justice

Temperance

Courage

Faith

Hope

Charity

Personal Prayer

Overcoming Vice Through the Grace of God

Pride

Greed

Lust

Envy

Gluttony

Wrath

Sloth

Personal Prayer

Read John 20:19-31 Christ's words to St. Thomas: Thomas was separated from the other apostles when Jesus had appeared to them before. Do you separate yourself through sin? Do you know people who do? Look at Jesus. Look at His wounds. Ask Him to help you overcome your faults. Pray for those who do not see Him that they, like Thomas, come to believe so that Christ's Church may flourish.

Virtue to Aquire

Predominant Fault to overcome

Because of my love for God I make these resolutions…

_____

_____

_____

_____

_____

_____

_____

_____

_____

Thank you Lord for…

Read John 6:27 Labour not for the meat which perisheth, but for that which endureth unto life everlasting. We Catholics know the severity of these words but how often do we listen and then allow ourselves to 'zone out' ?

Virtue to Aquire

Predominant Fault to overcome

Because of my love for God I make these resolutions…

_____

_____

_____

_____

_____

_____

_____

_____

_____

Thank you Lord for…

Read Matt 12:34. Out of the abundance of the heart the mouth speaketh. Read Ephes 4:29 Let no evil speech proceed from our mouth. If we break out into impatient and arrogant words or into injurious language we clearly have very little control over ourselves. How will we have strength in the awful days ahead to stand for our faith and Church. Pray, pray, knock, seek, ask for graces.

Virtue to Aquire

Predominant Fault to overcome

Because of my love for God I make these resolutions…

_____

_____

_____

_____

_____

_____

_____

_____

_____

_____

Thank you Lord for…

Read :Matt 5:12 For your reward is very great in heaven. For so they persecuted the prophets that were before you. How often do you feel friction with family, friends, or neighbours? When you do, quickly recall the friction Jesus felt at different times and join your hurt to His. Watch. Practice now over these simple things for the future brings much more devastating persecutions for Christians.

Virtue to Aquire

Predominant Fault to overcome

Because of my love for God I make these resolutions…

_____

_____

_____

_____

_____

_____

_____

_____

_____

_____

Thank you Lord for…

Read John 13:34 A new commandment I give you that you love one another as I have loved you. 1st. Putting up with others rudeness, ingratitude, anger, contradictions, moral defects, infirmity, depression. 2nd. Comforting them in temptation, counselling them in doubt. 3rd. Bearing part of their punishment due to their sins by praying for them and doing penance for them.

Virtue to Aquire

Predominant Fault to overcome

Because of my love for God I make these resolutions…

_____

_____

_____

_____

_____

_____

_____

_____

_____

_____

Thank you Lord for…

Read Matt 16:27. Then will he render to every man according to his works. How many people set out with great hopes of being saintly and soon become lukewarm? Unless we work every day every hour to overcome our faults and forgive others theirs what will be "rendered" to us after our death.

Virtue to Aquire

Predominant Fault to overcome

Because of my love for God I make these resolutions…

_____

_____

_____

_____

_____

_____

_____

_____

_____

_____

Thank you Lord for…

Read Matt 28:20 Behold I am with you always. Making progress in virtue: According to your situation in life you must advance in holiness but you cannot do this by yourself. First know your own weakness. Second you must frequently ask God for the graces to become better.

Virtue to Aquire

Predominant Fault to overcome

Because of my love for God I make these resolutions…

_____

_____

_____

_____

_____

_____

_____

_____

_____

Thank you Lord for…

Meditation Planner
Time & Place

Monday

Themes/focus:

Tuesday

Wednesday

Themes/Focus

Thursday

Friday

Notes:

Saturday

Meditation Planner
Time & Place

Monday

Themes/focus:

Tuesday

Wednesday

Themes/Focus

Thursday

Friday

Notes:

Saturday

Meditation Planner
Time & Place

Monday

Themes/focus:

Tuesday

Wednesday

Themes/Focus

Thursday

Friday

Notes:

Saturday

Meditation Planner
Time & Place

Monday

Themes/focus:

Tuesday

Wednesday

Themes/Focus

Thursday

Friday

Notes:

Saturday

Meditation Planner
Time & Place

Monday

Themes/focus:

Tuesday

Wednesday

Themes/Focus

Thursday

Friday

Notes:

Saturday

Meditation Planner
Time & Place

Monday

Themes/focus:

Tuesday

Wednesday

Themes/Focus

Thursday

Friday

Notes:

Saturday

St Teresa of Avila

St. Teresa of Ávila, also called Saint Teresa of Jesus, was born March 28, 1515, Ávila, Spain she died October 4, 1582 and canonized 1622; feast day October 15. Teresa was, one of the great mystics and religious women and author of spiritual classics. She was the originator of the Carmelite Reform, which restored and emphasised the austerity and contemplative character of primitive Carmelite life. .

St. Teresa

"To expedite our faults is our first objective in Mental Prayer"

"Although it appears to us that we have no imperfections, still when God opens the eyes of the soul, as He usually does in prayer, our imperfections are then clearly seen."

Before prayer, endeavour to realise Whose Presence you are approaching and to Whom you are about to speak, keeping in mind Whom you are addressing.

If our lives were a thousand times as long as they are we should never fully understand how we ought to behave towards God, before Whom the very Angels tremble, Who can do all He wills, and with Whom to wish, is to accomplish.

The soul must know and be conscious of God's love for it.

> "Majestic sovereign, timeless wisdom,
> your kindness melts my hard, cold soul.
> Handsome lover, selfless giver,
> your beauty fills my dull, sad eyes.
> I am yours, you made me.
> I am yours, you called me.
> I am yours, you saved me.
> I am yours, you loved me.
> I will never leave your presence.
> Give me death, give me life.
> Give me sickness, give me health.
> Give me honour, give me shame.
> Give me weakness, give me strength."
> I will have whatever you give. Amen

The First Commandment

Have you doubted in matters of faith? Consulted fortune-tellers? Believed in dreams? Made use of superstitious practices? Gone to places of false worship and taken an active part in the religious services of a false church? Belonged to Masons, Communists, of some other forbidden society? Read anti-Catholic books or papers? Neglected religious instruction? Omitted religious duties through fear or ridicule? Murmured against God, or despaired of His mercy? Have you rashly presumed on His goodness in committing sin? Did you pray in time of temptation? For your family? Have you neglected your daily prayers? Have you recited them carelessly, without devotion, thoughtlessly? Have you missed spending a reasonable amount of time in thanksgiving after Holy Communion? Have you been irreverent toward God, sacred persons, places or things? Have you associated with people who might have a bad influence upon your life? Have you refused to place signs of faith in your home, such as a crucifix, picture of the Blessed Mother or the saints?

The Second Commandment

Have you taken the name of God in vain? Laughed at the profane use of the name of God or irreverent speech by others? Given bad example to children by such speech in their presence, or by neglecting to correct a child when irreverent or profane language was used? Spoken disrespectfully of the saints or holy things? Allowed others in your household to do the same? Sworn falsely, that is, called upon God to witness the truth of what you were saying, when you were in reality telling a lie? Sworn rashly, or in slight and trivial matters? Have you cursed persons, animals, or things? Have you blasphemed, that is, used insulting language expressing contempt for God, His saints or sacred things? Have you caused others to do so? Have you criticized God's mercy or justice, or murmured against His providence?

The Third Commandment

Have you assisted at Mass on Sundays and Holy days? Have you been late for Mass? Behaved properly in Church? Have you performed or commanded unnecessary servile work, bought or sold without necessity, or in any other way – gambling, drinking – profaned these holy days?

The Fourth Commandment

Have you shown due honor, love, gratitude and obedience to your parents? Have you shown due honor and obedience to your pastors and other lawful superiors? Have you asked their pardon when you hurt them? Have you been disrespectful to your parents by speaking angrily to them, saying unkind, harsh words to them and about them, or by being ashamed of them?

If you are a parent, have you shown this lack of honor, love and gratitude to your parents in the presence of your children? Have you criticized them and rejected some of their orders? Have you corrected and punished your children for serious transgressions, or forbidden them to enter serious occasions of sin? Have you cooperated with teachers in the education of your children? Have you refused to send your children to Catholic school when you could have done so and had no permission from bishop or pastor to do otherwise? If there is no Catholic school in your vicinity, have you sent them to catechism faithfully?

Have you taken an interest in their catechism lessons? Have you cooperated with the Pastor and the Sisters in the projects sponsored by them to stimulate the children's interest in the faith? Have you trained and corrected your children in regard to chastity? Have you been disrespectful to aged persons? Have you had proper care for children and those dependent on you – both in physical and religious matters? Above all, have you given them a good example? If you are a child, have you refused to speak to your father or mother? Have you resented them? Have you disobeyed your parents when they gave you orders to avoid bad companions or dangerous occasions to sin? Have you obeyed the rules they made concerning persons to be brought into the house, the hours to be kept at night, or the conduct within the home?

When earning money, while living at home or while still subject to your parents, have you refused them part of your earnings when they needed it or demanded it? As a citizen, have you obeyed laws of the city and country made for the safety and well-being of all?

The Fifth Commandment

The fifth commandment forbids: Murder, suicide, criminal neglect that might cause serious injury or death to another, serious anger and hatred, abortion, mercy killing, the use of narcotics, sterilization, drunkenness, help extended to another to commit a mortal sin, fighting, anger, hatred and revenge.

Have you procured, desired, or hastened the death of any one? Have you been guilty of anger, hatred, quarreling, revenge? Used provoking language, insulting words, ridicule? Refused to speak to others? Caused enmities? Given scandal? Did you eat or drink too much? Have you been unkind, irritable, impatient? Have you provoked others to anger offended them, hurt them by anger or impatience? Have you entertained thoughts of jealousy, revenge, aversion, resentment or contempt of others? Have you kept company with those who drink to excess? Have you encouraged them to drink? Have you jested about their drunkenness?

Have you neglected your health or endangered your life? Have you neglected to take care of the health of your children or those subject to you? Have you endangered the life of others by driving an automobile while intoxicated or caused real danger to the safety of others in any other way?

The Sixth and Ninth Commandments
These two commandments demand purity and modesty in our life: in our thoughts, words, and actions, whether alone or with others.

In general, these commandments forbid: adultery, fornication, self-abuse, indecent dressing, necking, impure kisses, impure dancing, impure talk, sins against nature, birth control, impure touches, petting, looking at impure pictures, dances, movies, or reading impure books or magazines.

Have you been guilty of impure or immodest thoughts, words or actions – alone or with others? Have you spoken words or phrases of double meaning? Have you told suggestive stories? Have you encouraged others to do so? Have you taught others to do this? Have you avoided occasions of sin in this matter? Have you guarded your sight, or allowed your eyes to wander in curiosity over obviously dangerous objects? Have you put yourself in an occasion of sin by reading bad books, looking at indecent pictures, keeping bad company, attending immoral performances, watching indecent movies or television programs, singing lewd songs, and the like?

Have you distributed obscene books or magazines? Have you informed others of places of distribution? Have you encouraged others to read them? Have you desired to do impure things? Have you been an occasion of sin to others, by your conversation, dress, appearance, or actions? Have you touched yourself impurely? If you are married, have you committed sins of impurity with another married or single person? Taken part in prolonged kisses and embraces with others beside your partner in marriage?

Have you used contraceptive means in performing marriage duties? Have you, without good reason, refused or neglected to render the marriage obligation when seriously asked?

The Seventh and Tenth Commandments
These commandments forbid: robbery and burglary, graft, bribes, stealing and damaging the property of others.

These commandments forbid not merely stealing but every type of dishonest dealing, such as, cheating, unjust keeping of what belongs to others, unjust damage to property of others, graft on the part of public officials.

These commandments are also violated by merchants who use false weights, measures, who make exorbitant profits or lie about the essential qualities of their goods; by those who obtain money from others by persuading them to make unsound investments with the assurance of gain; by those who knowingly pass counterfeit money, or take undue advantage of the ignorance or necessity of another; by employers who defraud laborers; by employees who waste time during working hours, perform careless work or neglect to take reasonable care of the property of their employers; by employers who charge customers exorbitant prices; by those who do not return what they borrowed; by running up a charge account and not paying it; not returning found articles; selling articles with hidden defects for the usual price; not paying one's bills; by depriving one's family of necessities by gambling, drinking or foolish spending.

Have you stolen or retained ill-gotten goods? Damaged or wasted the property of others? Accepted bribes? Neglected to make restitution, or to help the poor? Have you desired the goods of others? Squandered their goods? As a parent, have you taught your children a strict sense of honesty and justice, punishing any slight theft or deceit? Have you sinned in any way mentioned above?

The Eighth Commandment
This commandment forbids: lies, calumny, detraction, perjury, unjust and unnecessary criticism, fault-finding, gossip, backbiting, insults, rash judgment, the telling of secrets one is bound to keep, cheating, tale-bearing.
Have you borne false witness for or against another? Been guilty of detraction, flattery, hypocrisy, lying, rash judgment?
Have you entertained unkind thoughts of others? Have you harbored suspicions, nursed resentments, refused to forgive others when they expressed their contrition? Have you spread unkind remarks others make to you? Do you discuss the faults of your parents, wife, husband, children with others who have no business knowing anything about them? At home are you given to nagging, complaining, arguing, refusing to talk, calling names, petty quarrelling?
Have you brought any harm to your neighbor and have you tried to repair it, as far as you were able? Have you tried to destroy the good work performed by another, or to hinder it seriously? Have you been sensitive, hurt, cool, thoughtless with others?

Saint Francis de Sales (1567-1622)

Born 21 August 1567. Died 28 December 1622 was a
Bishop of Geneva and is honoured as a saint in the Church.
He became noted for his deep faith and his gentle approach
to the religious divisions caused by the   Protestant
Reformation. He is known also for his writings on the topic
of spiritual direction and spiritual formation, particularly the
Introduction to the Devout Life and the *Treatise on the Love
of God*

Saint Francis de Sales tells us:

"Especially I commend earnest mental prayer to you, more particularly such as bears upon the Life and Passion of our Lord."

"If you contemplate Him frequently in meditation, your whole soul will be filled with Him, you will grow in His Likeness, and your actions will be moulded on His."

"Never be in a hurry; do everything quietly and in a calm spirit. Do not lose your inner peace for anything whatsoever, even if your whole world seems upset. What is anything in life compared to peace of soul?"

"Have patience with all things, but chiefly have patience with yourself. Do not lose courage in considering your own imperfections, but instantly set about remedying them— every day begin the task anew."

"If while saying vocal prayers, your heart feels drawn to mental prayer, do not resist it, but calmly let your mind follow that inclination. Do not be troubled because you have not finished your appointed vocal prayers."

Read John 10:11-16 As your Shepherd Jesus guides, feeds, and defends you. To be guided by Jesus you must follow in the virtues. Humility, patience, charity, meekness etc.

Virtue to Aquire

Predominant Fault to overcome

Because of my love for God I make these resolutions…

_____

_____

_____

_____

_____

_____

_____

_____

_____

Thank you Lord for…

Read John 10:9 I am the door. By me if any man enter in, he shall be saved; and he shall go in, and go out, and shall find pastures. Stand at the foot of the cross with Our Lady and go *in* to spirituality through Jesus; come *out* freely to the world and adore Him there as well.

Virtue to Aquire

Predominant Fault to overcome

Because of my love for God I make these resolutions…

_____

_____

_____

_____

_____

_____

_____

_____

_____

Thank you Lord for…

Read Matt. 18:9 If thy eye scandalise thee pluck it out, and cast it from thee. It is better for thee having one eye to enter into life, than having two eyes to be cast into hell fire. Do you allow freedom to your eyes. What do you watch? Would Our Lady sit with you watching it? Do you look with envy, does anger flash from your eyes?

Virtue to Aquire

Predominant Fault to overcome

Because of my love for God I make these resolutions…

_____

_____

_____

_____

_____

_____

_____

_____

_____

_____

Thank you Lord for…

Read Matt 6:5. Be not as the hypocrites that love to pray that they may be seen by man. Amen I say to you, they have received their reward. There are those who want great worldly praise but mostly this sin is committed in the heart where we sheepishly hope that friends, neighbours, the rest of the church sees our piety holiness!

Virtue to Aquire

Predominant Fault to overcome

Because of my love for God I make these resolutions…

_____

_____

_____

_____

_____

_____

_____

_____

_____

_____

Thank you Lord for…

Read John 14:26. The Holy Ghost, whom the Father will send in my name, he will teach you all things. "If any of you want wisdom, let him ask of God...and it shall be given him." James 1:5. Do you remember to turn for guidance to God in all difficulties FIRST?

Virtue to Aquire

Predominant Fault to overcome

Because of my love for God I make these resolutions…

_____

_____

_____

_____

_____

_____

_____

_____

_____

Thank you Lord for…

Read John 15:5 I am the vine, you the branches; he that abideh in me, and I in him, the same beareth much fruit, for without me you can do nothing. As branches need the trunk so we need Jesus as we 'grow out of Him'. It must be that close. No separation at all from Our Lord.

Virtue to Aquire

Predominant Fault to overcome

Because of my love for God I make these resolutions…

_____

_____

_____

_____

_____

_____

_____

_____

_____

_____

Thank you Lord for…

Read John 16:16-22 In a little while you shall see me. Jesus is telling us that we will suffer in this world but it will be worth it because we will see Him in heaven after the little while is over. Offer our daily sufferings to Him. Carry our crosses courageously. Do not complain or murmur. All pain will be forgotten when we see Jesus again.

Virtue to Aquire

Predominant Fault to overcome

Graces Received; Prayers Answered; Virtues Acquired

Thank you Lord for…

Read Luke 12:40 "Be you then also ready, for at what hour you think not, the son of man will come." The saints advise us to live each day as if it is our last. At first this seems depressing but what about paradise? Shouldn't we be so looking forward to it that we prepare each day to be ready if Jesus calls us home.

Virtue to Aquire

Predominant Fault to overcome

Because of my love for God I make these resolutions…

_____

_____

_____

_____

_____

_____

_____

_____

_____

_____

Thank you Lord for…

Brother Lawrence in the Practice
of The Presence of God explains:

"For the first years, I commonly employed myself during the time set apart for devotion with thoughts of death, judgment, hell, heaven, and my sins. Thus I continued some years applying my mind carefully the rest of the day, and even in the midst of my work, to the presence of God.

At length I began to do the same thing during my set time of prayer, which gave me joy and consolation. This practice produced in me so high an esteem for God that faith alone was enough to assure me."

Virtue to Aquire

Predominant Fault to overcome

Read Matt 5:30 "It is expedient for thee that one of thy members should perish rather than that thy whole body go into hell." We should care for our bodies but not let them become our master demanding every whim. Instead it should be employed for the benefit of our soul. In this health orientated world penance is abhorred like the plague of old.

Virtue to Aquire

Predominant Fault to overcome

Because of my love for God I make these resolutions…

_____

_____

_____

_____

_____

_____

_____

_____

_____

_____

Thank you Lord for…

Read John 7: 37-39. "If any man thirst, let him come to me and drink…
Now this he said of the Spirit which they should receive who believed in
him." You received streams of grace from the Holy Spirit that are supposed
to flow out into the world so that many other souls may drink of His grace
and come to know Jesus Christ.

Virtue to Aquire

Predominant Fault to overcome

Because of my love for God I make these resolutions…

_____

_____

_____

_____

_____

_____

_____

_____

_____

Thank you Lord for…

My Son, I must be thy Supreme and final end, if thou desirest to be truly happy. Out of such purpose thy affection shall be purified, which too often is sinfully bent upon itself and upon created things. For if thou seekest thyself in any matter, straightway thou wilt fail within thyself and grow barren. Therefore refer everything to Me first of all, for it is I who gave thee all. So look upon each blessing as flowing from the Supreme Good, and thus all things are to be

Virtue to Aquire

Predominant Fault to overcome

Because of my love for God I make these resolutions…

_____

_____

_____

_____

_____

_____

_____

_____

_____

_____

Thank you Lord for…

"This is the Truth, and by it the vanity of boasting is put to flight. And if heavenly grace and true charity shall enter into thee, there shall be no envy, nor longings of the heart, nor shall any self-love take possession of thee. For divine charity conquers all things, and enlarges all the powers of the soul. If thou art truly wise, thou wilt rejoice in Me alone, thou wilt hope in Me alone; for there is none good but one, that is God, Who is to be praised above all things, and in all things to receive blessing."

Virtue to Aquire

Predominant Fault to overcome

Because of my love for God I make these resolutions…

_____

_____

_____

_____

_____

_____

_____

_____

_____

_____

Thank you Lord for…

"To place thy desire altogether in subjection to My good pleasure, and not to be a lover of thyself, but an earnest seeker of My will. Thy desires often excite and urge thee forward; but consider with thyself whether thou art not more moved for thine own objects than for My honour. If it is Myself that thou seeks, thou shalt be well content with whatsoever I shall ordain; but if any pursuit of thine own lies hidden within thee, behold it is this which hinderers and weighs thee down.

Virtue to Aquire

Predominant Fault to overcome

Because of my love for God I make these resolutions…

_____

_____

_____

_____

_____

_____

_____

_____

_____

_____

Thank you Lord for…

"Sometimes, indeed, it is needful to use violence, and manfully to strive against the sensual appetite, and not to consider what the flesh may or not will; but rather to strive after this, that it may become subject, however unwillingly, to the spirit. And for so long it ought to be chastised and compelled to undergo slavery, even until it be ready for all things, and learn to be contented with little, to be delighted with things simple, and never to murmur at any inconvenience."

Virtue to Aquire

Predominant Fault to overcome

Because of my love for God I make these resolutions…

_____

_____

_____

_____

_____

_____

_____

_____

_____

Thank you Lord for…

"My Son, speak to me in every matter, 'Lord, if it please Thee, let this come to pass. Lord, if this shall be for Thine honour, let it be done in Thy Name. Lord, if thou see it good for me, and approve it as useful, then grant me to use it for Thy honour. But if you know that it shall be hurtful unto me, and not profitable for the health of my soul, take the desire away from me'! For not every desire is from the Holy Ghost, although it appear to a man right and good. It is difficult to judge with certainty whether a good or an evil spirit move thee to desire this or that, or whether thou art moved by thine own spirit. Many have been deceived at the last, who seemed at the beginning to be moved by a good spirit.

Virtue to Aquire

Predominant Fault to overcome

Because of my love for God I make these resolutions…

Thank you Lord for…

Saint Catherine of Siena.

Born 25 March 1347, died 29 April 1380, Catherine was a laywoman associated with the Dominican Order. She was a mystic, and author. Canonized in 1461, she is also a Doctor of the Church.

"God is closer to us than water is to a Fish"

"Ponder the fact that God has made you a gardener, to
root out vice and plant virtue."

"Nothing great is ever achieved without
much enduring"

"Build yourself a cell in your heart
and retire there to pray."

"Strange that so much suffering is caused because of
the misunderstandings of God's true nature. God's
heart is more gentle than the Virgin's first kiss upon
the Christ. And God's forgiveness to all, to any
thought or act, is more certain than our own being."

"My Son! I came down from heaven for thy salvation; I took upon Me thy miseries not of necessity, but drawn by love that thou might learn patience and might bear temporal miseries without murmuring. For from the hour of My birth, until My death upon the Cross, I ceased not from bearing of sorrow; I had much lack of temporal things; I oftentimes heard many reproaches against Myself; I gently bore contradictions and hard words; I received ingratitude for benefits, blasphemies for My miracles, rebukes for My doctrine."

Virtue to Aquire

Predominant Fault to overcome

Because of my love for God I make these resolutions…

_____

_____

_____

_____

_____

_____

_____

_____

_____

_____

Thank you Lord for…

What sayest thou, My Son? Cease to complain; consider My suffering and that of My saints. Thou hast not yet resisted unto blood.(1) It is little that you suffer in comparison with those who have suffered so many things, have been so strongly tempted, so grievously troubled, so many wise proved and tried. Thou ought therefore to call to mind the more grievous sufferings of others that thou might bear thy lesser ones more easily, and if they seem not to thee little, see that it is not thy impatience which is the cause of this. But whether they be little or whether they be great, study to bear them all with patience.

Virtue to Aquire

Predominant Fault to overcome

Because of my love for God I make these resolutions…

_____

_____

_____

_____

_____

_____

_____

_____

_____

_____

Thank you Lord for…

O Lord my God, be not Thou far from me, my God, haste Thee to help me, for many thoughts and great fears have risen up, afflicting my soul. How shall I pass through them unhurt? how shall I break through them? "I, will go before thee, and make the crooked places straight. I will open the prison doors, and reveal to thee the secret places.

Virtue to Aquire

Predominant Fault to overcome

Because of my love for God I make these resolutions…

_____

_____

_____

_____

_____

_____

_____

_____

_____

_____

Thank you Lord for…

"My Son, thou canst not possess perfect liberty unless thou altogether deny thyself. All they are enslaved who are possessors of riches, they who love themselves, the selfish, the curious, the restless; those who ever seek after soft things, and not after the things of Jesus Christ; those who continually plan and devise that which will not stand. For whatsoever cometh not of God shall perish. Hold fast the short and complete saying, 'Renounce all things, and thou shalt find all things; give up thy lust, and thou shalt find rest.' Dwell upon this in thy mind, and when thou art full of it, thou shalt understand all things."

Virtue to Aquire

Predominant Fault to overcome

Because of my love for God I make these resolutions...

_____

_____

_____

_____

_____

_____

_____

_____

_____

_____

Thank you Lord for...

Enlighten me, Blessed Jesus, with the brightness of Thy inner light, and cast forth all darkness from the habitation of my heart. Restrain my many wandering thoughts, and carry away the temptations which strive to do me hurt. Fight Thou mightily for me, and drive forth the evil beasts, I call alluring lusts, that peace may be within Thy walls and plenteousness of praise within Thy palaces, even in my pure conscience. say to sea, "Be still," say to the stormy wind, "Hold thy peace," so shall there be a great calm.

Virtue to Aquire

Predominant Fault to overcome

Because of my love for God I make these resolutions…

_____

_____

_____

_____

_____

_____

_____

_____

_____

_____

Thank you Lord for…

CONTEMPLATION

Meditation in the Catholic vocabulary is the reading and seeking a deeper understanding of scripture or the things pertaining to God and His kingdom. In Meditation we speak to God but all the work is on our side. We actively seek understanding. Meditation is that enhancement of Jesus' advice ask seek and knock. All our efforts in Mediation are to look into the scriptures asking God for His guidance and knowledge. We use our imagination to conjure up a profound appreciation of the life of Our Lord.

Mental Prayer which is often the fruit of our Meditation is when our meditation turns into what is called by the saints an intimate conversation with God. And here God speaks back with His Spiritual voice. He sheds light on our soul. We come right up to the narrow gate and seek admittance. But wait we are not slender enough to get through. All that baggage. Those dark thoughts dark intentions - they present in the spiritual world as huge bulbous appendages stuck to our frame. We are too large, filled up with ourselves. A camel could get through more easily than we.

And so God shows us where we need to make adjustments to our spiritual life, starting in the material world with our motives, thoughts, behaviours. This is Mental Prayer.

Contemplation often evolves from Mental Prayer. God takes over. There is silence.
God "invades" the soul, We do nothing except BE in the all pervasive presence.

We become nothing God is ALL.

The saints tell us that Contemplation does not come quickly because if God were to take us to the heights of contemplation immediately we might get too attached to it and miss out on the first important steps. As we begin the journey towards Him we would expect this grace all the time and truthfully we may not be mature enough to handle it sensibly.

CONTEMPLATING ON THE ATTRIBUTES OF GOD
NOTES

Contemplation

is nothing else but a
secret, peaceful, and
loving infusion of God,
which, if admitted,
will set the soul on fire
with the Spirit of love.

John of the Cross

Place your mind before the mirror of eternity. Place your soul in the brilliance of glory! And transform your entire being into the image of the Godhead itself through contemplation. Clare of Assisi

On the following pages are listed the Attributes of God. Choose one to focus your meditation and use the three pages for notes on graces received.

ON THE ATTRIBUTES OF GOD

His Wisdom. His Goodness.
His Power. His Majesty. His Glory.
His Greatness. His Immensity.
His Infinity. …

ON THE ATTRIBUTES OF GOD
His Eternity. His Holiness His Justice.
His Mercy. His Clemency. His Patience.
His Sweetness. His Providence. ...

ON THE ATTRIBUTES OF GOD
His Benignity. His Fidelity. His Beauty.
His Beatitude. His Peace. His Light.
He is Redeemer. He is Sanctifier.
He is Creator;

"My Son! walk before Me in truth, and in the simplicity of thy heart seek Me continually. He who walks before Me in the truth shall be safe from evil assaults, and the truth shall deliver him from the wiles and slanders of the wicked. If the truth shall make thee free, thou shalt be free indeed, and shalt not care for the vain words of men."

Virtue to Aquire

Predominant Fault to overcome

Because of my love for God I make these resolutions…

_____

_____

_____

_____

_____

_____

_____

_____

_____

_____

Thank you Lord for…

He who is not ready to suffer all things, and to conform to the will of the Beloved, is not worthy to be called a lover of God. It benefits him who loves God to embrace willingly all hard and bitter things for the Beloved's sake, and not to be drawn away from Him because of any contrary accidents

Virtue to Aquire

Predominant Fault to overcome

Because of my love for God I make these resolutions…

_____

_____

_____

_____

_____

_____

_____

_____

_____

Thank you Lord for…

I will teach thee," saith the Truth, "the things which are right and pleasing before Me. Think upon thy sins with great displeasure and sorrow, and never think thyself anything because of thy good works. Verily thou art a sinner, liable to many passions, yea, tied and bound with them. Of thyself thou wilt quickly fall, quickly be conquered, quickly disturbed, quickly undone. Thou hast nought whereof to glory, but many reasons why thou shouldest reckon thyself vile, for thou art far weaker than thou art able to comprehend.

Virtue to Aquire

Predominant Fault to overcome

Because of my love for God I make these resolutions…

_____

_____

_____

_____

_____

_____

_____

_____

_____

_____

Thank you Lord for…

Son, be not curious, nor trouble thyself with vain cares. What is that to thee? Follow thou Me. For what is it to thee whether a man be this or that, or say or do thus or thus? Thou hast no need to answer for others, but thou must give an answer for thyself. Why therefore dost thou entangle thyself? Behold, I know all men, and I behold all things which are done under the sun; and I know how it stands with each one, what he thinks, what he wills, and to what end his thoughts reach. All things therefore are to be committed to Me; watch thyself in godly peace, and leave him who is unquiet to be unquiet as he will. Whatsoever he shall do or say, shall come unto him, for he cannot deceive Me.

Virtue to Aquire

Predominant Fault to overcome

Because of my love for God I make these resolutions…

_____

_____

_____

_____

_____

_____

_____

_____

_____

Thank you Lord for…

"My Son, thou must give all for all, and be nothing of thine own. Know that the love of thyself is more hurtful to thee than anything in the world. According to the love and inclination which thou hast, everything more or less cleaves to thee. If thy love be pure, sincere, well-regulated, thou shalt not be in captivity to anything. Do not covet what thou mayest not have; do not have what is able to hinder thee, and to rob thee of inward liberty.

Virtue to Aquire

Predominant Fault to overcome

Because of my love for God I make these resolutions…

_____

_____

_____

_____

_____

_____

_____

_____

_____

_____

Thank you Lord for…

Give me, O Lord, heavenly wisdom, that I may learn to seek Thee above all things and to find Thee; to relish Thee above all things and to love Thee; and to understand all other things, even as they are, according to the order of Thy wisdom. Grant me prudently to avoid the flatterer, and patiently to bear with him that opposes me; for this is great wisdom, not to be carried by every wind of words, nor to give ear to the wicked flattering Siren; for thus do we go safely on in the way we have begun

Virtue to Aquire

Predominant Fault to overcome

Because of my love for God I make these resolutions…

Thank you Lord for…

My Son, take it not sadly to heart, if any think ill of thee, and say of thee what thou art unwilling to hear. Thou ought to think worse of thyself, and to believe no man weaker than thyself. If you walk inwardly, you will not weigh flying words above their value. It is no small prudence to keep silence in an evil time and to turn inwardly unto Me, and not to be troubled by human judgment.

Virtue to Aquire

Predominant Fault to overcome

Because of my love for God I make these resolutions…

_____

_____

_____

_____

_____

_____

_____

_____

_____

Thank you Lord for…

"My Son, I the Lord am a stronghold in the day of trouble.
Come unto Me, when it is not well with thee.

Virtue to Aquire

Predominant Fault to overcome

Because of my love for God I make these resolutions…

_____

_____

_____

_____

_____

_____

_____

_____

_____

_____

Thank you Lord for…

Virtue to Aquire

Predominant Fault to overcome

End Notes

He who does not meditate acts as one who never looks into the mirror and so does not bother to put himself in order, since he can be dirty without knowing it.

The person who meditates and turns his thoughts to God who is the mirror of the soul, seeks to know his defects and tries to correct them, moderates himself in his impulses and puts his conscience in order. Padre Pio

Quotes researched from:
www.AZQuotes.com.
goodreads.com/author/quotes

St John of the Cross Dark Night of the Soul
St Teresa of Avila Interior castle.
St Frances de Sales Introduction to the Devout Life.

www.traditionalcatholicpriest.com

https://www.britannica.com/biography/Saint-Teresa-of-Avila

Made in the USA
Las Vegas, NV
05 January 2024

83957747R00121